A Wind from God

A Wind from God

Prayers for Recovery
from Hurricane Katrina

Barbara Booth Hemphill

Shadow Verse Press
Kingwood, Texas

Shadow Verse Press, Kingwood, Texas 77345
www.shadowverse.com

Printed in the United States of America

13 12 11 10 09 08 07 06 05   1 2 3 4 5

ISBN: 0-9761931-1-6

Front Cover and Insert Photos: NASA/ Jeff Schmaltz,
                    MODIS Land Rapid Response Team

I am indebted to the United States news media for their
reporting from New Orleans in the aftermath of Katrina. Some
of their stories are reflected in these meditations. *The New York
Times* article "Macabre Reminder: The Corpse on Union Street"
by Dan Barry (September 8, 2005) was an inspiration for this
book.

**Proceeds from sales of this book will be donated
to the Bush-Clinton Katrina Fund.**

To St. Rita

and

the Sisters of St. Joan

Contents

Foreword

Hurricane Katrina ripped across the Gulf Coast August 29, 2005. Mississippi, Alabama, and Louisiana felt the blast of 145 mph winds. Massive tidal surges vaporized almost everything near the shore. But New Orleans was spared the brunt of the winds when the storm veered slightly to the east. Then the levees broke, and water from Lake Pontchartrain began pouring into the city.

The rest of the nation watched the disaster unfold as people struggled to survive for days without medication, without food, without potable water. The people of New Orleans and the Gulf Coast were traumatized, losing so much so quickly. We who witnessed it on television were also deeply wounded, knowing we were powerless to aid the suffering we so clearly observed.

A Wind from God: Prayers for Recovery from Hurricane Katrina attempts to create a climate conducive to healing these wounds, by helping the reader connect the story of the storm with the deep story of the Christian faith. It includes forty meditations modeled on the ancient practice of Lectio Divina, holy reading.

Each meditation begins with an excerpt from a scripture passage in which water plays a central role. The scripture reading is followed by a poem stanza relating one dimension of the Katrina story, in the voice of a participant in the New Orleans area. The meditation closes with a brief prayer weaving together the sacred text and the poem, creating a new and personal faith story.

The meditations are intended to serve as examples, though I hope they offer something beneficial on their own terms. I invite you to journal your own Lectio Divina experiences with these same scripture readings (using the entire passage rather than the quoted excerpt), following the method outlined in "How to Use This Book." Two sample journaling pages are included near the end of the book.

My husband and I lived in New Orleans almost fourteen years. Our son grew up there; he considers the Big Easy his home town. So in my own small way, I am a survivor too. I pray that reading and journaling with *A Wind from God* becomes a source of healing for you, as writing it has been for me.

Barbara Booth Hemphill
October 15, 2005
Feast Day of St. Teresa of Avila

How to Use This Book

The meditations in *A Wind from God* are founded on the ancient Christian practice of Lectio Divina — a meditative reading of sacred texts that listens for present-moment meanings and connections. Lectio Divina is a receptive activity that opens the heart to God's self-communication through the words and images of scripture. It is a transforming devotional exercise with four steps or dimensions.

The first step is to read the *entire* scripture passage slowly, listening for a word, phrase, or image that calls for your attention. This becomes the word through which you expect to hear God speak today.

Next, read the passage again. Spend some time letting that word, phrase, or image connect with your life. Repeat it inwardly, slowly, meditatively. Look at the image in your mind. Relax. Allow it to draw to itself your memories of Katrina, or other life storms. Allow yourself to feel and sense whatever is connected with those memories.

Then, standing in the midst of those connections and memories, ask God for what you need in that place. Or, turning it around, ask what God is offering you there. What is God inviting you to do or become? This is your prayer.

Finally, spend a few minutes in silence, resting in God's love for you in the midst of those memories, that need, that holy invitation.

For Small Groups

In individual practice, the four stages of Lectio Divina may flow easily into one another. They may be experienced as complementary aspects of one prayer, rather than steps in a clear process.

In group practice, the Lectio Divina stages may be more defined. For example, after reading the text aloud the first time, and a couple of minutes of silence, the facilitator invites group members to share (if they choose to) only the *word, phrase, or image* that drew their attention. Then the text is read aloud a second time, followed by a few more minutes of silence, and an opportunity to share *connections and memories*. Then there is a third reading of the text, silence, and sharing of the *prayer* that emerged. The group practice ends with a few minutes of silence.

Another way to do Lectio Divina in a group is to read the text twice in the beginning, and then allow ten to twenty minutes of silence. During the silence, group members find their *word*, experience *connections*, and locate a *prayer*. Then there is a single opportunity for people to share a summary of their experience, followed by a few minutes of silent prayer to conclude the exercise.

During Lent

The forty meditations would be appropriate for a Lenten retreat or for personal Lenten devotions.

In the Beginning … Darkness

In the beginning when God created the heavens and the earth, the earth was a formless void and darkness covered the face of the deep, while a wind from God swept over the face of the waters.

— Genesis 1:1-3

It was dark when the storm arrived,
and darker still after it left.
First was the dark of night;
then came the dark of death.

Holy Wind, sweep over the face of the waters,
the deluge that flooded homes and hearts,
leaving us formless and void.
Speak light in our darkness.

Entering the Ark

Noah with his sons, Shem and Ham and Japheth, and Noah's wife and the three wives of his sons entered the ark … They went into the ark with Noah, two and two of all flesh in which there was the breath of life.
— *Genesis 7:11-16*

With Katrina two days away
we gathered family, pets, and treasures,
beginning our exile in haste,
with no goodbyes.

God of Fountains and Rain,
when water sends us far from home,
surround us with loved and loving creatures
filled with the breath of life.

When the Water Was Gone

When the water in the skin was gone, she cast the child under one of the bushes ... And as she sat opposite him, she lifted up her voice and wept.

— *Genesis 21:14-19*

Our few days' supply was exhausted,
and so were we. My children's thirst
was more than my eyes could bear.
I could see nothing else.

God of the Outcast, send us
to the lonely, the abandoned, the hopeless,
to children who thirst,
helping them find resources to survive.
Make us wells in their wilderness.

3

The River Stank

All the water in the river was turned into blood, and the fish in the river died. The river stank so that the Egyptians could not drink its water.

— *Exodus 7:20-24*

As hours and days dragged by,
the constant stench grew worse.
Surrounded by water unfit to drink
and heat that kindled thirst.

Wonderworking God, you showed your power
by turning the Nile to blood, making it stink.
Reverse your power today:
Pour your fragrance through this fetid city;
Cleanse Lake Pontchartrain.
Give us leaders, staffs, miracles of purification.

Driven Back by an East Wind

The Lord drove the sea back by a strong east wind all night, and turned the sea into dry land; and the waters were divided ... Thus the Lord saved Israel that day from the Egyptians.

— Exodus 14:15-30

We dreamed of deliverance
when Katrina was driven east,
giving thanks to God, levees and pumps
for dry ground and streets.

God of Wind and Sea, give us gratitude
for temporary deliverance
from the destructive forces of nature.
Teach us to use the safe time well.

They Found No Water

They went three days in the wilderness and found no water ... And the people complained against Moses saying, "What shall we drink?"

— Exodus 15:22-25

We waded to the Superdome —
our last resort, our home for days.
Chaos, heat, thirst, waste, and no supplies;
We complained, "When will help arrive?"

God of the Wilderness, when you lead us
to emptiness and desolation
we are lost, but even there you are God,
making the bitterness sweet.
Help us to wait with patience and hope.

Why Did You Bring Us Out?

They camped at Rephidim ... But the people thirsted there for water; and the people complained against Moses and said, "Why did you bring us out of Egypt, to kill us and our children and livestock with thirst?"

— Exodus 17:1-6

We thought they had abandoned us
to thirst and hunger,
castaways on inner city islands,
out of sight and further out of mind.

God our Rock,
you hear our complaints as infant cries
for necessities deeper than we know.
Grant us your ears
and your providing heart.

The Bronze Basin

The Lord spoke to Moses: You shall make a bronze basin with a bronze stand for washing. You shall put it between the tent of meeting and the altar, and you shall put water in it.

— Exodus 30:17-20

After the levees broke,
water filled the basin
between us and anywhere.
The bowl that is New Orleans bathed us all.

Purifying God, wash our hands and feet,
contaminated by their meeting
with polluted waters.
Heal us by your washing,
that we may not die.

The Dust of the Golden Calf

*He took the calf that they had made, burned it with fire,
ground it to powder, scattered it on the water, and made
the Israelites drink it.*

— Exodus 32:15-20

The flood, the fires, the scattering,
seemed like Judgment Day.
The city that poured hurricanes
was made to drink a murky, bitter cup.

God of Tablets, whole and broken,
you forgive our constant calf-making,
our dancing to discordant melodies.
Help us to drink with grace
the cup set before us, and forgive.

Crossing the Jordan

When those who bore the ark had come to the Jordan, and the feet of the priests bearing the ark were dipped in the edge of the water, the waters flowing from above stood still ... Then the people crossed over opposite Jericho.
— Joshua 3:14-17

With Harry Connick, Jr. we came from Baton Rouge
to cover victims' stories for "Today."
We crossed the Mississippi at the GNO Bridge;
We never met a puddle on our way.

God of the Covenant, lead us by a dry path
into abundant life.
Give us leaders willing to get their feet wet,
followers willing to cross the river,
and the wisdom to know the difference.

Sifting the Troops

Then the Lord said to Gideon, "The troops are still too many; take them down to the water and I will sift them out for you there."

— Judges 7:4-7

Many of our troops, our Guard,
had been deployed for duty in Iraq.
Those who remained assisted with the
search and rescue efforts round the clock.

Sifting God, you accomplish great things
with meager means.
When to our eyes the tool
seems smaller than the task,
give us confidence in your possibilities.

His Spirit Returned

By then he was very thirsty, and he called on the Lord …
So God split open the hollow place that is at Lehi, and
water came from it. When he drank, his spirit returned,
and he revived.

— Judges 15:18-19

We huddled in Convention Center heat
as the first of the supply trucks arrived.
Camouflaged angels slaked our thirst;
I knew we would survive.

Reviving God, you meet our deepest needs,
bringing life to body and spirit at once.
Teach us to see and address others' needs
as equally spiritual and physical.

Rescued from the Waters

*The cords of Sheol entangled me, the snares of death con-
fronted me ... He reached down from on high, he took me,
he drew me out of mighty waters.*

— 2 Samuel 22:1-17

When the waters rose, we scrambled
to the attic, then the roof,
painting signs of life on shingles
for the helicopters sent to our rescue.

Most High God, in this era of flight
people and machines reach down
to do your work, to rescue from certain death.
Protect the rescuers and their flying machines.

The Water is Bad

Now the people of the city said to Elisha, "The location of this city is good, as my lord sees; but the water is bad, and the land is unfruitful." ... "Thus says the Lord, I have made this water wholesome ..."

— 2 Kings 2:19-22

I have nightmares —
water overflowing everything,
rising, pursuing, as I run in fear.
Katrina haunts me.

God of fruitfulness,
cleanse our hurricane memories.
Turn these painful experiences to our good
and the good of all your people and the earth.

Immersed Seven Times

Elisha sent a messenger to him, saying, "Go, wash in the Jordan seven times, and your flesh shall be restored and you shall be clean."

— 2 Kings 5:10-14

Seven days wading through streets
seeking survivors in need of supplies,
seven immersions in life's dark waters —
my week with New Orleans police.

Cleansing God,
we risked our own lives to save others,
immersing ourselves in death for the sake of life.
Honor our sacrifice with healing.

His Ax Head Fell Into the Water

When they came to the Jordan, they cut down trees. But as one was felling a log, his ax head fell into the water ... Then the man of God ... made the iron float.
— *2 Kings 6:4-7*

I worked at a refinery in Chalmette,
spent days off with friends
and tools in my garage.
Katrina and the water took them all.

Saving God, restore what we have lost --
jobs, friends, hobbies,
and the means to pursue them.
Make our lives float,
so we can pick them up again.

Who Shut in the Sea?

Then the Lord answered Job out of the whirlwind: " ... Or who shut in the sea with doors when it burst out from the womb?"

— Job 38:1, 8-11

When Betsy struck in 1965
we constructed bars and doors
sixteen feet high, to hold the lake,
to say "Thus far ... no farther" to the waves.

God of the Whirlwind, you restrained the sea
at the creation of the earth, blessing the land.
Help us to construct doors and bars,
levees and gates, that protect our homes
and honor nature's power.

Beside Still Waters

The Lord is my shepherd, I shall not want. He makes me lie down in green pastures; he leads me beside still waters; he restores my soul.

— Psalm 23

We buried my mother last month
in Metairie Cemetery.
After the winds had died, I waded
to her tomb to measure the water line.

Shepherd of Souls, you walk with us
through the valley of death.
Grant peace to the living
when even the dead are drowned.

Deep Calls to Deep

Deep calls to deep at the thunder of your cataracts; all
your waves and your billows have gone over me. By day
the Lord commands his steadfast love, and at night his
song is with me, a prayer to the God of my life.
— Psalm 42:7-8

Thunder of Katrina's cataract,

the levee at the 17th Street Canal,

caused a sudden downrush in my bones,

a marrow-dwelling fear: my life was gone.

God of the Deep,
even in the night your song is with us.
When the music of life is silent,
help us sing from the depth of our hearts,
from the marrow of our bones.

My Eyes Grow Dim with Waiting

*Save me, O God, for the waters have come up to my neck
… I am weary with my crying; my throat is parched. My
eyes grow dim with waiting for my God.*

— *Psalm 69:1-3*

The waters quickly rose up to our necks;
too weak to run, too frail to hold it back.
St. Rita's intervention was delayed.
Our cause is lost, and yet, "St. Rita, pray…"

God our Vision, we wait, parched and weary,
hoping blindly for your saving intervention.
Help us attend to the needs of the ill and old,
the weak and frail, bringing ordinary love
until your extraordinary power arrives.

When the Waters Saw You

When the waters saw you, O God, when the waters saw you, they were afraid; the very deep trembled ... The crash of your thunder was in the whirlwind; your lightnings lit up the world; the earth trembled and shook.

— Psalm 77:16-19

I moved to New Orleans from New York.
Never had I seen a hurricane.
My first would be this category five.
Regardless of its path, I was terrified.

Almighty God, earth's storms
are but a shadow of your power.
Yet seeing them, we tremble with fear.
Turn our fear to awe,
our terror to reverence and peace.

My Companions are in Darkness

Your dread assaults destroy me. They surround me like a flood all day long; from all sides they close in on me. You have caused friend and neighbor to shun me; my companions are in darkness.

— Psalm 88:16-18

My neighbors left before the storm.
I stayed. Katrina scattered friends
like seeds to distant fields,
companions in exile, threshed by wind.

Loving God, grant us friends
who understand the pain of exile,
companions in darkness.
Help us to sprout in these new fields.

I Have Called You by Name

Do not fear, for I have redeemed you; I have called you by name, you are mine. When you pass through the waters, I will be with you; and through the rivers, they shall not overwhelm you.

— Isaiah 43:1-2

On the day you took my name
I promised to protect you,
to be with you as long we would live.
But when the water took you, I let go.

You were with us when the waters parted us.
Now I alone survive,
overwhelmed with grief and guilt.
God, forgive. God, redeem.
God, call my name again.

Buy Without Money

Ho, everyone who thirsts, come to the waters; and you
that have no money, come, buy and eat! Come, buy wine
and milk without money and without price.

— *Isaiah 55:1-3*

The stores were closed, everyone gone;
No cashiers, no security guards.
Broken windows became doorways;
we went in and took what we needed.

Generous God, you invite us
to your well-supplied table,
where without fear of starvation
our grasping ends. Grant us entrance
into your priceless abundance.

A River That I Could Not Cross

Again he measured one thousand, and it was a river that
I could not cross, for the water had risen; it was deep
enough to swim in, a river that could not be crossed.
— Ezekiel 47:1-5

He kept coming to get us,
one after the other, leading us to safety.
Each time the water was deeper.
I was last, and I could not swim.

God of the Temple,
you measure the depth and breadth
of all things, seen and unseen.
When we cannot cross life's rivers,
deep enough to swim in, carry us.

Justice and Righteousness

Take away from me the noise of your songs; I will not listen to the melody of your harps. But let justice roll down like waters, and righteousness like an everflowing stream.

— Amos 5:18-24

Why were the poor left behind
when the water rolled down to the city?
No car and no place in the minds
of the evacuation committee.

Just and Righteous God,
you desire mercy more than sacrifice.
Fill our lives and our religious rites
with compassion, with active love,
for the poor.

Three Days in a Big Fish

The waters closed in over me; the deep surrounded me …
Then the Lord spoke to the fish, and it spewed Jonah out
upon the dry land.

— Jonah 2:3-10

Three days in the Dome, no power;
Three days, and it smells like fish.
Then here comes a bus to take some of us
on a Houston-bound pilgrimage.

God Who Speaks to Fish,
you deliver us from the deep
and move us to dry land.
Yet even on dry land
the flood surrounds us.
Keep speaking.

A Voice from Heaven

And just as he was coming up out of the water, he saw the heavens torn apart and the Spirit descending like a dove on him. And a voice came from heaven, "You are my Son, the Beloved; with you I am well pleased."

— Mark 1:9-11

I thought I heard your voice.
No, maybe it was thunder.
So many years, the silence;
I doubt my ears, but not the reassurance.

Voice of Heaven, in the storm
it is hard to believe
that you are pleased with us.
As we recover, reassure us
of your good pleasure and your love.

Fill the Jars with Water

Jesus said to them, "Fill the jars with water." And they filled them up to the brim. He said to them, "Now draw some out, and take it to the chief steward."
— *John 2:1-11*

Before the storm they filled all their containers.
Then suddenly they left, not locking doors.
We waded through the house in search of bodies
but found the gift of water in their jars.

Jesus our Vine, you supply the best wine
in quiet ways, behind the scenes,
through people and means
we do not understand or know.
Help us to appreciate the random acts of kindness
that grace our lives.

A House Unshaken

That one is like a man building a house, who dug deeply and laid the foundation on rock; when a flood arose, the river burst against that house but could not shake it, because it had been well built.

— Luke 6:47-49

The mayor said to evacuate; we did.
Some friends in Alexandria took us in.
Our house withstood the flood,
but everything we left inside became a ruin.

Christ our Sure Foundation,
standing through the flood was not enough.
Though on the outside we appear to be okay,
we are ruined within, stained by the muck.
Act on your words; dig deeply; heal us.

Give Me a Drink

A Samaritan woman came to draw water, and Jesus said to her, "Give me a drink."... Jesus said to her, "Everyone who drinks of this water will be thirsty again, but those who drink of the water that I will give them will never be thirsty."

— John 4:7-15

I get so tired of standing in these lines,
waiting for water in the heat of the day.
A bottle barely satisfies my thirst.
I don't have any left to give away.

Jesus, you thirsted twice —
first in Samaria, then on the cross.
You know the power of human need
and the limits of human generosity.
Help us trust in your eternal supply,
your spring.

Sleeping Through the Storm

A windstorm arose on the sea, so great that the boat was being swamped by the waves; but he was asleep ... Then he got up and rebuked the winds and the sea; and there was a dead calm.

— Matthew 8:23-26

Babies can sleep through anything!
Wind howled; raindrops exploded on glass.
My grandson dozed in peace
until the dead calm brought its heat.

Lord of Wind and Sea,
we cannot sleep for fear.
When windstorms swamp our little boats
grant us peace in mystery,
the living calm of faith.

The Healing Pool

Now in Jerusalem by the Sheep Gate there is a pool, called in Hebrew Bethzatha, which has five porticoes. In these lay many invalids — blind, lame, and paralyzed.
— John 5:2-9

We evacuated patients from Charity
to Tulane (they share a helipad) —
first those in ICU and then the rest.
But snipers put a halt to our good work.

Christ the Healer, you made the blind see,
the deaf hear, the lame dance.
When our healing work is assaulted
by lack of power and by violence,
encourage us, work through us,
help us stand and walk.

It Is a Ghost!

But when the disciples saw him walking on the sea, they were terrified, saying, "It is a ghost!" And they cried out in fear.

— Matthew 14:25-27

Why didn't I cry out, or gasp at least,
seeing the corpse on Union Street?
Katrina has kidnapped my heart and drowned
its human care beneath her waves.

Jesus, you comforted your disciples,
telling them not to be afraid.
My lack of fear haunts me
more than ghosts or honest terror.
Rescue my heart, so I can take it back.

On the Last Day

On the last day of the festival, the great day, while Jesus was standing there, he cried out, "Let anyone who is thirsty come to me, and let the one who believes in me drink. As the scripture has said, 'Out of the believer's heart shall flow rivers of living water.'"

— John 7:37-39

On the last day of our searching,
less for life and more for bodies to recover,
a muffled shout within an old man's home!
He'd lived two weeks on a single jug of water.

Living Water, we have imbibed
miraculous rescues and tragic deaths.
We thirst for ordinary life,
with its commonplace disasters and salvations.
Flow through our hearts your river of quiet grace.

Mud in the Eye

As he walked along, he saw a man blind from birth ... He spat on the ground and made mud with the saliva and spread the mud on the man's eyes, saying to him, "Go, wash in the pool of Siloam" (which means Sent). Then he went and washed and came back able to see.

— John 9:1-7

I went back with my family to Gentilly.
The neighborhood was caked in mud;
all that we owned, lost to the flood.
I spat on the damp ground and closed my eyes.

Mud Maker,
you created Adam from the earth,
and healed with mud the man blind from his birth.
Heal us through this caked mud
and through the washing;
recreate us with fresh sight conceived in dirt.

Washing Feet

"Do you know what I have done to you? ... If I, your Lord and Teacher, have washed your feet, you also ought to wash one another's feet. For I have set you an example, that you also should do as I have done to you."
— *John 13:1-5, 12-15*

I ended up in Denver in a shelter.
They took us all in buses to a spa.
That pedicure did more than soothe my feet;
its cool and fragrant balm consoled my heart.

Foot Washing God, you serve us,
stooping down to touch our feet,
so stained by earth.
Grant us grace to follow your example,
trusting in the healing power
of this humble work.

I Am Innocent

So when Pilate saw that he could do nothing, but rather
that a riot was beginning, he took some water and washed
his hands before the crowd, saying, "I am innocent of this
man's blood; see to it yourselves."

— *Matthew 27:24-26*

It seemed that no one took responsibility.
Tales of snipers, rapes, and looting;
The film noir that we were shooting
couldn't match the gloom of this reality.

God who suffered at the hands of innocence,
help us claim our influence, our power,
both to prevent harm and to do good,
seeking pardon rather than perfection,
offering confession rather than excuse.

Already Dead

So they asked Pilate to have the legs of the crucified men broken and the bodies removed ... But when they came to Jesus and saw that he was already dead, they did not break his legs.

— John 19:31-34

When we saw that he was already dead
we painted orange letters on the door.
"1-D" we wrote; we covered him and left.
Removing him was someone else's chore.

God of the Living, your people's death
is precious in your sight.
When reverence for life requires
abandoning the dead,
accept our paint as prayer
our covering as eulogy and rite.

Tree of Life

On either side of the river, is the tree of life with its twelve kinds of fruit, producing its fruit each month; and the leaves of the tree are for the healing of the nations.
— Revelation 22:1-5, 17

I worry about trees. They can't evacuate.
Thousands in City Park must be near death,
under feet of standing water many days.
How long can a live oak hold its breath?

God Who Heals Through Trees,
you entrust us with the care of your creation.
As we aid our ancient oaks,
make us into living leaves
for the heailng of this city and the nations.

Title / Page: _____

Word, phrase, or image:

Connections, memories:

Prayer (Request or Response to Invitation):

Title / Page: _____

Word, phrase, or image:

Connections, memories:

Prayer (Request or Response to Invitation):

Sample Journal Page

Publisher Notes

Donation of publisher's profits:

Shadow Verse Press will donate its profits from sales of *A Wind from God* to the Bush-Clinton Katrina fund.

See www.bushclintonkatrinafund.org for more information, or to make a donation for the rebuilding of Louisiana, Mississippi, and Alabama.

Also from Shadow Verse Press:

Magellan's Shadow: Faith Poems (2004)
ISBN: 0-9761931-0-8
2005 Independent Publisher Book Award
     (IPPY) -- Finalist in Poetry.

For more information see our web site, www.shadowverse.com.

Contact us / Book orders:

Shadow Verse Press
3719 Clover Creek Dr
Kingwood, TX 77345

info@shadowverse.com
barbara@shadowverse.com (the author)

This is powerful and beautifully written. She is a marvelous poet. Her thoughts hit you and stick!

Nina L. Diamond
Independent Publisher magazine
Judge, 2005 IPPY Awards

Shadow Verse Press (2004)
www.shadowverse.com

Paperback: 104 pages

ISBN: 0-9761931-0-8

Book Dimensions:
8.8 x 6.0 x 0.29 inches

Magellan's Shadow: Faith Poems

From the Author, Barbara Booth Hemphill

An important part of being a spiritual director, a chaplain, or just a good listener, is accompanying people in pain, confusion, despair. You have to be at home in the dark, able to walk with people without knocking over their inner furniture or turning on the lights, so to speak. The only way I know to be that kind of companion in darkness is to be at peace with my own shadows. The poems in *Magellan's Shadow* were written as I tried to find that peace within myself. As I wrote them, I found myself moving from a black-white world to a world where light embraces darkness.